RED FOX

THAT'S SO GROSS! HISTORY
A RED FOX BOOK 978 1 849 41189 9

Published in Great Britain by Red Fox,
an imprint of Random House Children's Books
A Random House Group Company

This edition published 2011

1 3 5 7 9 10 8 6 4 2

The Random House Group Limited supports the Forest Stewardship Council (FSC), the leading international forest certification organization. All our titles that are printed on Greenpeace-approved FSC-certified paper carry the FSC logo. Our paper procurement policy can be found at www.rbooks.co.uk/environment.

Set in Optima

RANDOM HOUSE CHILDREN'S BOOKS
61–63 Uxbridge Road, London W5 5SA

www.kidsatrandomhouse.co.uk
www.rbooks.co.uk

Addresses for companies within The Random House Group Limited can be found at:
www.randomhouse.co.uk/offices.htm

THE RANDOM HOUSE GROUP Limited Reg. No. 954009
A CIP catalogue record for this book is available from the British Library.

Printed in the UK by CPI Bookmarque, Croydon, CR0 4TD

To all fans
of truly
GROSS trivia!

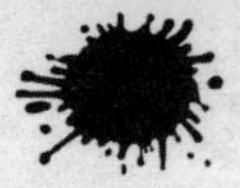

INTRODUCTION

Welcome to a brand-new series of books which all have one thing in common: they're all intended to be ENGROSSING – with the emphasis on the third, fourth, fifth, sixth and seventh letters.

I've selected facts that are particularly gruesome in the hope that you will be disgusted and entertained in equal measure. Occasionally – very occasionally – I have used a fact from one of my other books (there's a list on page two but my editor and I know them fondly as 'Bum', 'Bogeys', 'Poo', 'Farts', Ear Wax', 'Puke' and 'Loos'. I've only done this where it fits in so perfectly that *not* to do it would be even worse!

There are three other books in this series. If you get them all, then you'll know as much as I do – or, indeed, *more* because as soon as I discover a new fascinating fact, I promptly forget at least two old ones! I think my brain's storage section has reached its full capacity.

As usual, I have a lot of thank yous. The most

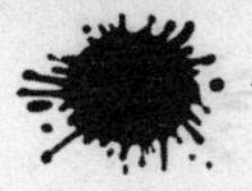

important people were (in alphabetical order): Nigel Baines, Lauren Buckland, Penny Chorlton, Dominica Clements, Annie Eaton, Charlie Symons and Jack Symons.

In addition, I'd also like to thank the following people for their help, contributions and/or support: Gilly Adams, Luigi Bonomi, Paul Donnelley, Jonathan Fingerhut, Jenny Garrison, Bryn Musson, Mari Roberts, Louise Symons and Rob Woolley.

As I always write at this point, if I've missed anyone out, then please know that – as with any mistakes in the book – it is, as ever, entirely down to my own stupidity.

Mitchell Symons

www.mitchellsymons.co.uk
www.grossbooks.co.uk

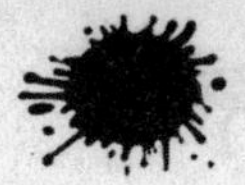

ENGROSSING LIVING

Be glad that you weren't a child in England in the Middle Ages, for if you were, you'd have been sewn into your clothes for the entire winter. This was because it was never warm enough to take them off – even in bed – and, of course, there was no central heating! The clothes would only be taken off in the spring.

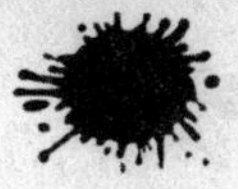

But however grim life might have been for English children in the Middle Ages, it was a lot *lot* worse for Chinese girls until the twentieth century. This is because of the practice of footbinding.

You see, small feet were considered beautiful, with the foot seen as an extension of the leg rather than as a stand for the body. So the Chinese would restrict the growth of their feet to prevent them growing any longer than about eight centimetres.

The whole process would begin when a girl was young – supposedly so that the feet would be easier to mould, but the truth is that the practice didn't involve moulding as much as it did breaking. All the toes on each foot (except for the big toes) were *broken* and folded under the sole, and then the toes were bound in place with a silk or cotton bandage.

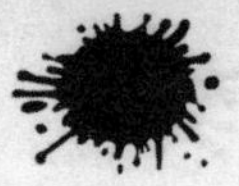

The dressings were removed every two days to allow the washing of the toenails to avoid infection. Immediately afterwards the bandages would go back on – tighter and tighter still. Eventually the arches of the feet would also be broken so that feet could be pulled straight with the legs.

There were professional footbinders who, unlike the girls' mothers, didn't care how much pain the girls suffered. And the pain would have been excruciating – especially as the girls weren't allowed to rest after their feet had been bound. Instead, they were made to walk on their broken and bound feet so that their body weight would help them crush their feet into the desired shape.

Eventually they'd 'achieve' this shape, but because their feet would keep on growing, they'd have to endure ten more years of footbinding. Not only was it painful, it was

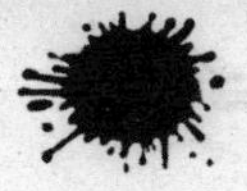

also life-threatening. Toes would fall off because the blood couldn't get to them and toenails would cut into the feet and cause infection leading to gangrene and, sometimes, death. Even when women survived such ghastly infections, their feet would effectively 'die' – leaving a horrible smell that would accompany the woman for the rest of her life. And all for fashion!

In prehistoric times, the average person lived to the age of eighteen.

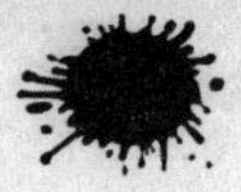

Have you heard the expression 'to wear a hairshirt'? It means to punish yourself excessively for your faults. It comes from the practice by certain very religious people of wearing a rough undergarment made of sackcloth or coarse animal hair that would be very uncomfortable, the idea being that it would expel sin and make the wearer pious and faithful . . . Thomas Becket, a twelfth-century Archbishop of Canterbury, wore a hairshirt that he refused to take off. After he died – murdered on the wishes (if not the orders) of King Henry II – they found his hairshirt was crawling with lice.

Fashionable medieval Italian women used the highly poisonous deadly nightshade plant in their make-up routine. Putting the juice of the plant in their eyes made the pupils enlarge, an effect regarded as very attractive. This led to the plant's Latin name, Belladonna, which means beautiful woman. Prolonged use could make the user go blind . . .

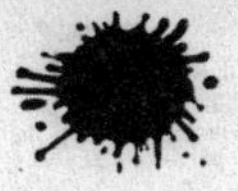

Medieval women would use sulphur to burn off freckles. However, probably nothing did as much harm as the poisonous lead preparations that women in Elizabethan and later times routinely used as their foundation. It made their faces very white, which was not only fashionable but also masked things like smallpox scars.

The ancient Romans used pigeon droppings to lighten their hair – ghastly, but not altogether stupid as the ammonia in the droppings would certainly have acted as a bleach.

In 1358, there were only four public toilets in the whole of London. These weren't toilets as we would understand them, but places where people could do what they had to do straight into a river or cesspit. The largest 'toilet' was on London Bridge and it emptied straight into the River Thames.

A popular (male) activity in the Middle Ages was for two people to bash each other with wooden clubs. Yup, you can see why television had to be invented. Known as 'cudgel play', two combatants would fight each other with wooden clubs (cudgels). The first person to make his opponent bleed was the winner.

James Lucas – also known as the Hermit of Hertfordshire – was a Victorian eccentric who became internationally famous as 'the dirtiest man in England'. Because he never washed, his body went black with grease and grime.

Interestingly, he wasn't a pauper but a well-educated landowner who had studied medicine and was a good conversationalist. However, after his mother's death in 1849, he became a complete recluse and barricaded himself into his home – living only in the kitchen and sleeping on a bed of ashes and soot. Of course, his house became infested with rats and he kept his food in baskets hung from the ceiling to protect it from them. Lucas communicated with the world through an iron grille but was perfectly happy to receive visitors – including Charles Dickens. After Lucas's death in 1874, 17 cartloads of dirt and ashes were removed from the house.

In ancient Rome, there was a tradition of nailing a dead owl, with its wings outspread, above a door to ward off any approaching storms.

The Huns – a warlike nomadic people who

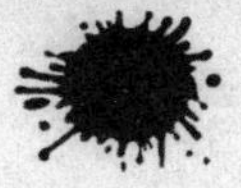

lived in Germany and eastern Europe from the fourth to the sixth centuries – used to cut boys' faces – just to make them look tougher. Actually, so scary were Hun leader Attila and his followers that in the twelfth century, the Magyar people decided to cash in on everyone's fear of them by naming their country *Hun*gary – on the basis of some remote connection to the Huns.

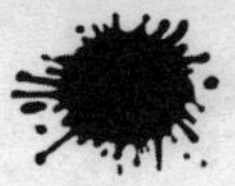

In Greenland it used to be fashionable for women to paint their faces blue and yellow.

In the Middle Ages, people used to place *live* cats in the walls of new houses to keep out evil spirits.

'What's the worst job you ever had?' is a question that people of my age often ask of one another. Mine was shelf-stacking in a supermarket when I was a kid. But that's nothing compared to being a slave of the Roman Emperor Claudius. He held feasts that required so much eating that guests would regularly have to throw up in order to be able to carry on. And the slaves' job? That's right. They had to help the guests puke. *Not* fun . . .

Viking warriors used to make blood pacts with each other. They would cut their hands or arms and mix their blood with the blood of a fellow warrior. Sometimes, they'd do that and then thrust their bloody hands into the soil so their mixed blood would be part of the earth. Of course in those days they hadn't heard of tetanus . . .

In Sparta, children were only allowed to bathe three times a year. No wonder we still

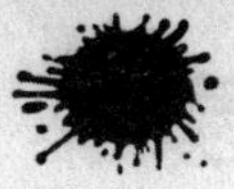

use the word 'spartan' to describe facilities that are extremely basic!

In ancient Greece, they used to predict the future by examining the entrails (insides) of dead birds. I say 'predict' but I very much doubt that they were successful in their predictions!

New Scythian soldiers had to drink the blood of the first enemy soldier they killed. They also had to collect the scalps of the people they killed in order to claim a share of the loot after a battle. The more scalps, the more loot.

When medieval Europeans burned witches, their families had to pay for the firewood.

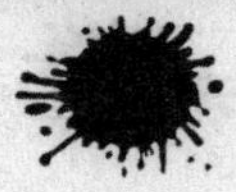

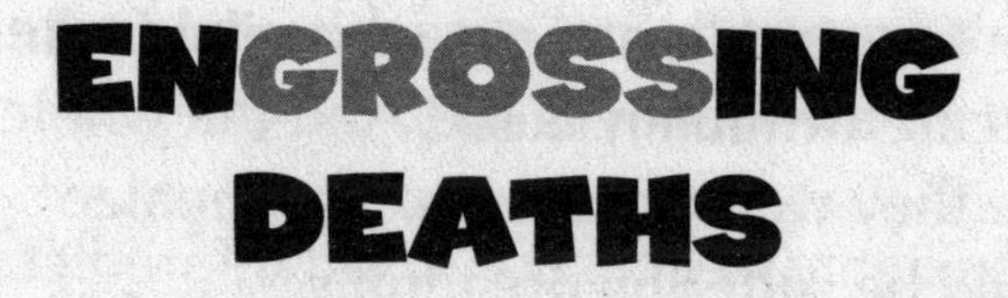

ENGROSSING DEATHS

Vlad the Impaler was an extremely cruel man (the clue's in the name) so it's not surprising that his enemies were pretty cruel themselves. In 1447, they killed him and then took his eldest son (and heir), blinded him with hot iron stakes and then buried him alive. But you won't blame these people when I tell you how Vlad got his infamous nickname. He impaled thousands of people during his reign – sometimes just for stealing a loaf of bread. But mainly Vlad impaled people – especially captured soldiers – to inspire fear in his enemies.

In case you were wondering, impaling means to spit someone onto a spike. It was NOT a quick death. If the spike or a stick

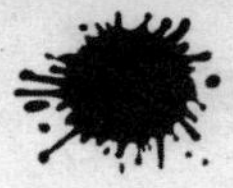

didn't rupture a vital organ, it could take days for the victim to die. And the whole time they were conscious, the impalee would be suffering dreadfully.

Aeschylus, an ancient Greek playwright, is said to have died when an eagle passing overhead dropped a tortoise on his head.

King Henry I died in 1135 after eating 'a surfeit of lampreys' (that's too many eels to you and me). He was in Normandy at the time and so they had to get him home – not an easy thing to do with a rotting corpse on a journey taking many days. So they took his remains and put them into the skin of a bull. The skin was then sewn up and he was taken back to England and buried at Reading Abbey, which he himself had founded fourteen years before.

Talking of English kings' corpses – as we were – I have to tell you about William

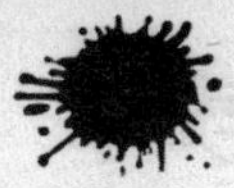

the Conqueror (or William I as he became after 1066 and all that) who died in 1087. Unfortunately, his body was too big for his coffin. So two soldiers were ordered to stand on the body to squeeze it in. This they

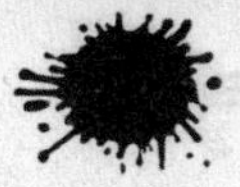

did with so much vigour – jumping up and down on it – that they caused his stomach to explode with a loud bang. Apparently, the resulting smell was so awful that the whole building had to be evacuated.

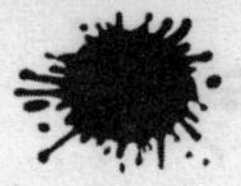

One person who would have been extremely amused by that story (if he hadn't himself died fifteen years earlier) was Hereward the Wake. From his base in the Isle of Ely, he resisted William and his Norman invading army and fought against them in Cambridgeshire, Lincolnshire and Norfolk. One day, he came home from fighting to find his brother's head nailed over the door of his family's house. He took down his brother's head and, that very same night, cut off the heads of some Norman soldiers and nailed *them* over the door instead.

In 260AD, the Roman Emperor Valerian was captured and subjected to humiliating treatment by the Persians – for example, they used him as a human footstool. Eventually, it has been claimed, they killed him by pouring molten gold down his throat. That sounds like a pretty rich death to me!

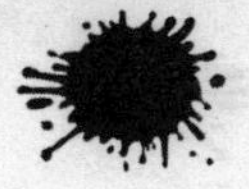

Ivan the Terrible – once again the clue's in the name – ruled Russia with a lot of cruelty. This even extended to his own family. In 1581, he decided that his daughter-in-law wasn't dressed suitably and so he beat her – despite the fact that she was pregnant. When her husband (Ivan's son) found out, he had a row with his father. Not unreasonably you might think – but it turned out to be a bad move as Ivan beat his son to death with a spiked stick.

In ancient China, people would commit suicide by eating a pound of salt.

In the eighteenth and nineteenth centuries, people in Britain – including children – were hanged for trivial offences. In 1819, Thomas Wildish was hanged for letter-stealing; in 1750, Benjamin Beckonfield was hanged for stealing a hat; in 1833, an unnamed nine-year-old boy was hanged for stealing a pennyworth of paint from a shop; in 1782, a

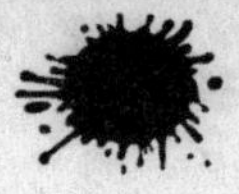

14-year-old girl was hanged for being found in the company of gypsies.

In 1736, Thomas Reynolds was hanged for robbery at Tyburn. He was cut down and placed in a coffin. However, as the hangman's assistant was putting on the lid, it was pushed away and the assistant's arm was grabbed from within. Reynolds was taken out of the coffin and to a nearby house, where he vomited three pints of blood and died.

Around 100AD, as a punishment for being a Christian, St Ignatius of Antioch was transported from Turkey to Rome and then thrown to the lions in the Colosseum. Not surprisingly, the lions ripped him apart!

How horrid is your mother? Does she make you eat up all your vegetables? Does she sometimes send you to bed early because you've been naughty? Well consider yourself

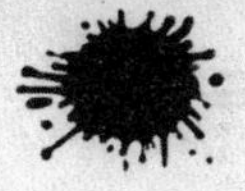

lucky. The Byzantine emperor Constantine VI, who reigned from 780–797, had a mother who would win *any* Worst Mother In The World contest. She wanted to be in charge of the empire so she ordered her own soldiers to capture her son and then blind him. He died from his injuries. What an evil woman! She's one person who'd have no right to complain if she didn't get a Mother's Day card.

In 1016, the Saxon king Edmund II was killed by a Viking who was hiding in the toilet (or, to be more accurate, the pit over which poor old Edmund was about to sit down), and killed him by stabbing him in the bottom.

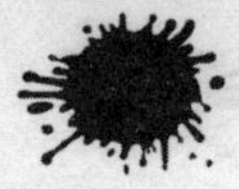

Gerolamo Cardano was an Italian astrologer who predicted that he would die in 1576. Just to make sure his prediction would be right . . . he killed himself that very year. Gerolamo wasn't the only colourful character in the Cardano family. His eldest

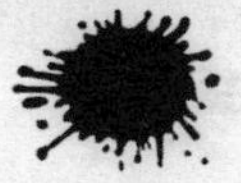

(and favourite) son was executed after murdering his wife, and another son was a gambler, who stole money from him. How did he punish him? It is said that he cut off the boy's ears.

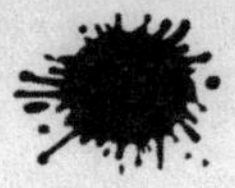

In the fourteenth century, the Aztecs ruled the land that we now know as Mexico. They used to sacrifice people (typically their captives) by, literally, tearing out their hearts while they were still alive.

In 897, Pope Stephen VI accused former Pope Formosus of crimes against the church. Unfortunately for Pope Stephen, Pope Formosus had died nine months earlier. So Stephen exhumed his body, dressed it in full papal regalia and put it on trial. As chief prosecutor, he then cross-examined the corpse. Er, yes, you read that right . . . *he cross-examined the corpse*.

Pope Stephen VI was of course absolutely stark raving bonkers. Nuttier than a family of hazelnuts eating peanut butter sandwiches at a festival of nuts. He was also an ungrateful lunatic because Pope Formosus was the man who'd made him a bishop in the first place.

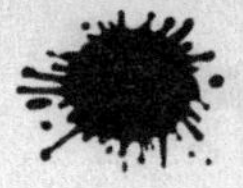

Anyway, Formosus – or, rather, his corpse – was found guilty, stripped of his sacred vestments, deprived of three fingers of the right hand (the blessing fingers), put in ordinary clothes, and buried. For good measure, it was then re-exhumed and thrown in the River Tiber. However, before Stephen could bask in his victory, his colleagues came to the same conclusion that we did two paragraphs ago: that he was totally potty and an excellent candidate for the puzzle factory.

So they duly locked him up and then, for extra good measure, strangled him to death. Then they reversed Formosus's conviction – which was all very well, but a bit meaningless in any event – and that's where this extraordinary story ends.

The 1666 Great Fire of London was popularly believed to have been started by 'papists and foreigners'. Robert Hubert, a

French watchmaker from Rouen, France was arrested. He 'confessed' (i.e. was tortured) and was hanged. Yet, according to Captain Peterson, the Master of the ship that had brought Hubert to London, he hadn't left the ship until two days *after* the fire had started.

The Celts also sacrificed people. Their method involved placing them inside a giant wooden statue of a god and then burning the statue – with the person in it – to the ground.

In 1159, Pope Adrian IV, the only Englishman ever to be pope, choked to death after a fly got stuck in his throat as he was taking a drink from a glass of wine.

A man attempted to assassinate Queen Mary I by climbing St James's Palace and using a large lens to focus the sun's rays on her while she was walking below. It failed . . .

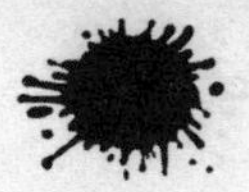

In China in the tenth century, a relative of the emperor was accidentally killed during a game of polo. The emperor's response was to have the entire opposing team beheaded.

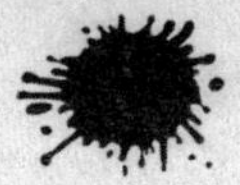

Queen Supayalat of Burma, the last queen of Burma (1878–1885), was determined to protect her husband, the king. So she reputedly ordered a hundred of his relations to be massacred – just to make sure they didn't try to take his throne away from him.

In 1789, Catherine Murphy officially became the last British woman to be sentenced to execution by burning. Except she wasn't actually burned! Let me explain. Catherine Murphy was convicted of making counterfeit coins – along with a lot of other people, including her husband. But because they were all men, they were sentenced to hang; as a woman, she was sentenced to be burned at the stake. Here's what happened though. She was brought out past the hanging bodies of her co-defendants and made to stand on a small platform in front of the stake where she was secured with ropes. A fire was set at the bottom of the stake. But

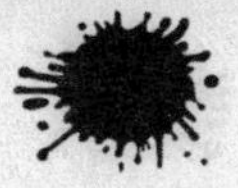

at this point, according to witnesses, she was hanged instead, the fire not being lit until after she was dead. The next year, burning as a method of execution was abolished.

Vlad the Impaler – the ruler of Wallachia (present day Romania) from 1456 to 1462 – was infamous for his cruelty. When 55 Turkish ambassadors refused to remove their hats in his presence he had their hats nailed to their heads.

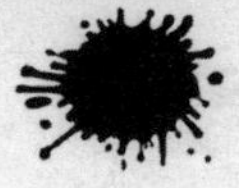

Similarly, the last British man sentenced to be hanged, drawn and quartered, also wasn't hanged, drawn and quartered! In 1803, Edward Despard was found guilty of high treason, despite Lord Horatio Nelson appearing in court as a character witness on his behalf. His sentence would have meant him being hanged by the neck but taken down before he was dead. Then he would have had his entrails (his inner body parts) 'drawn' from his body and burned in front of him – if he hadn't already died from the shock of it all. Finally, he would have been beheaded and his body would have been 'quartered' into pieces. This was the very punishment meted out to Sir William Wallace, the Scottish rebel leader, five hundred years earlier. However, in Despard's case, the authorities were worried that the public might protest if he got the full h., d. and q. treatment and so he was 'merely' hanged and then beheaded – in front of a

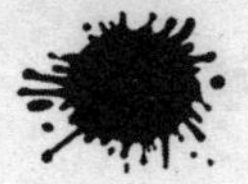

crowd of at least 20,000 people.

Another person sentenced to be hanged, drawn and quartered was Guy Fawkes – because of his involvement in the 1605 Gunpowder Plot. However, Guy escaped the drawing and quartering by jumping off the scaffold during the hanging and breaking his neck.

Here's a novel way of killing someone. In 1287, Kublai Khan, a grandson of the truly cruel Genghis Khan, wanted to kill his uncle, a rival to his throne. So what did he do? Poison him? Strangle him? Behead him? Nah, all too boring for Krazy Kublai. Instead, he had him wrapped in a carpet and then thrown around until he died. This ensured he didn't spill any royal blood. Who'd have thought it?

In 1531, the Bishop of Rochester's cook was sentenced to death for allegedly poisoning members of the bishop's household. He was

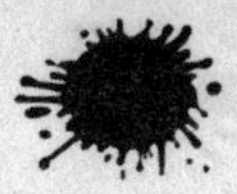

taken to the town square where he was put into a pot of cold water hanging over a fire. It took two hours for the water to boil and kill him.

In 1680, Manfredo Settala became the only person in all recorded history to have been killed by a meteorite.

Defenestration is a grisly way to go. Defene . . . what? Defenestration. It's the act of throwing someone out of a window

and it gets its name from the Latin words meaning 'out of' and 'window'. The first recorded defenestration was several years before the word was even invented! In the Bible, Jezebel was defenestrated by her own servants.

Common causes of death can change over time. Look at this list from the register of deaths (1893–1907). Nowadays, nearly all of these conditions are treatable – especially the bacterial infections, which can be cured very simply with antibiotics.

Abscess: A collection of pus, in any part of the body, usually due to injury or infection from bacteria
Appendicitis
Brain fever
Bright's Disease: Kidney disease
Bursting of blood vessel
Childbirth
Child's cough
Cholera

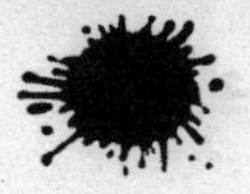

Concussion
Convulsions
Croup: Terrible cough and difficulty in breathing
Diarrhoea
Diphtheria: Breathing disease caused by bacteria
Dropsy: Unnatural accumulation of fluid in bodily tissues
Dysentery: Diarrhoea with fever and ulceration of the large intestine
Epilepsy
Exhaustion
Fits: Used to describe strokes, convulsions or anything leading to unconsciousness and death
Gas of stomach
General debility: Another catch-all word for when the doctor couldn't come to a particular diagnosis
Indigestion
Infection in bladder

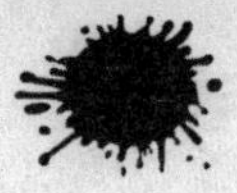

Insanity: Almost impossible to die from insanity itself, so it was presumably used in cases where someone who had previously been diagnosed as insane, died of an unspecified disease or accident
Insomnia: Prolonged inability to sleep properly
Lockjaw: A type of tetanus in which the jaws are locked rigidly together; trismus
Obstruction of bowels
Scarlet fever: So called because of the scarlet rash that usually appears on the second day
Teething
Vertigo: Dizziness

In 1839, an American man was hanged for the murder of his wife. So far, nothing remarkable. However, while he was awaiting execution, he sold his body to the prison doctors. Again, not unusual: they would have used it to further their knowledge of anatomy. They gave him 10

dollars, of which he spent nine on goodies to eat. Just as he was about to be executed, he realized that he still had a dollar bill in his pocket. So he asked for a couple of slices of bread, put the note in it and ate a one-dollar sandwich.

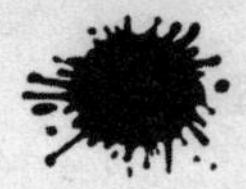

ENGROSSING - INTERESTING

Slavery ended in France a lot earlier than it did in other countries – and all because of a woman named Balthild. As a young girl, she was sold into slavery in France and attracted the attention of King Clovis. They married in 649AD and when her husband died, she abolished the practice of slave-trading and actively worked to free children who'd been sold into slavery. Interestingly, when her three sons grew up, she renounced her royal status and dedicated the rest of her life to looking after the poor and sick. Not surprisingly, she was made a saint some two hundred years after her death. What a wonderful woman – so what is she doing in a book like this? Oh well, it makes a refreshing change!

Back to reality . . . In the fifteenth century, Queen Isabella of Castille famously boasted of having bathed only twice in her entire lifetime.

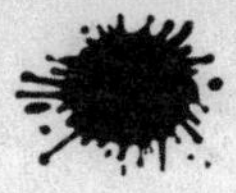

by Dr Jean-Baptiste Denis, physician to King Louis XIV. He transfused 12 ounces of lamb's blood into a young boy who had been bled using leeches. Incredibly, the boy survived. Samuel Pepys describes a similar treatment for a Cambridge student, Arthur Coga, who agreed to have 20 ounces of sheep's blood transfused into his body. After the transfusion Pepys noted that, 'he is a little cracked in his head, though he speaks very reasonably'. To be fair, he had been described as 'the subject of a harmless form of insanity' before the procedure.

When Adolf Hitler saw a pile of bricks near the church of St Matthew in Munich, Germany, he said, 'That pile of stones will have to be removed.' Of course, whenever Hitler spoke, people rushed to carry out his every whim. Unfortunately, they got it wrong and thought he was referring to the church (rather than to the pile of stones) and so they demolished it.

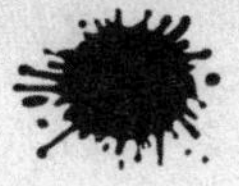

Lady Jane Grey was queen of England for just nine days in 1553 – hence her nickname 'The Nine-Day Queen'. Here's how it happened. When Henry VIII died, his son Edward became king. Edward had two half-sisters: Mary (later Mary I) and Elizabeth (later Elizabeth I). As Protestant Edward lay dying – at the age of just fifteen – he was persuaded by courtiers anxious to bypass the Catholic Mary to instead make his Protestant cousin Jane, queen. This he did, however Mary managed to rally her supporters and have Jane deposed. She then became queen. As for poor Lady Jane, who herself was only 17 years old, she was sentenced to death. As an act of kindness, this was changed from burning at the stake in public to a beheading in private.

Sir Isaac Newton was probably the most important mathematician and physicist in our history. However, that's not how he finds his way into this book. No, we prefer to remember him as a child when he once

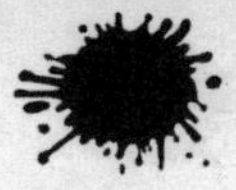

made a list of his sins. These included squirting water, punching his sister, making pies on a Sunday, and wishing to burn his mother and stepfather 'and the house over them'.

When the ancient Egyptians made mummies out of their dead, they took out the brain and threw it away, and removed the innards and put them in jars. They also removed the eyes and replaced them with stones – or onions!

During World War I, soldiers were constantly on their guard against gas attacks. The best defence was a purpose-made gas mark, but if one wasn't available, they would pee on a handkerchief and then cover their faces with it.

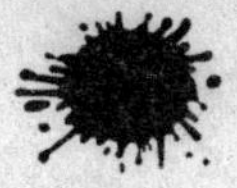

The famous seventeenth-century Italian astronomer, Galileo Galilei, spent so much time looking at the sun with his telescope that he was blind for the last four years of his life.

In 1883, the eruption of Krakatoa put so much dust into the atmosphere that global temperatures dropped by more than a degree centigrade and for the next two years the moon appeared blue.

The Battle of Waterloo was fought in 1815. The British commander, the Duke of Wellington, and the French leader, Napoleon Bonaparte, were probably the equal of each other when it came to their battle tactics and their respective forces. So why did Wellington win? Well, it could have something to do with the fact that Napoleon had a sore bottom on the day. It's true – I'm not kidding you. He had a bad case of piles – lumps in the . . . oh go and ask your mum or

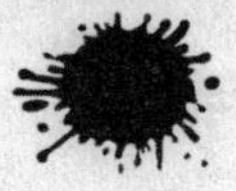

dad – and that meant he couldn't sit on his horse to survey the battlefield and that's why the French lost the Battle of Waterloo.

Talking of Napoleon, he had a drinking cup made out of the skull of a famous Italian explorer named Cagliostro.

The body of Admiral Nelson was preserved in a barrel of brandy.

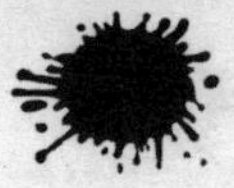

The remains of Alexander the Great were preserved in a huge vat of honey.

In 1191, the English king Richard the Lionheart was laying siege to the city of Acre during the Third Crusade. He ordered his men to throw loads of beehives over the walls of the besieged city. This did the trick and the people surrendered immediately.

In the nineteenth century, doctors were desperate for human corpses so that they could study anatomy through dissection (cutting up bodies). Two rogues named William Burke and William Hare decided to supply an Edinburgh anatomy lecturer named Robert Knox by killing people and selling him the bodies. They killed seventeen people before they were eventually caught.

Because the evidence against them wasn't that good, Hare was offered a deal: testify against his former partner and be spared the death penalty. So he did. Burke was hanged in 1829 after which he was – fitting ending alert – publicly dissected at the Edinburgh Medical College.

You might be interested to know that some of Burke's skin was circulated to ghoulish collectors. Charles Dickens had a piece of it and used it as a bookmark.

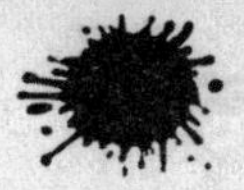

When, later in her reign, Queen Elizabeth I had lost all her teeth, she filled out her mouth with cloth whenever she went out in public. Well, you've got to keep up appearances!

When a British ship arrived at a port in China, it did what ships often did back then in the nineteenth century, it fired its cannon as a form of greeting. Unfortunately, someone on the shore who was watching the ship's arrival was killed. To avoid a diplomatic incident, the ship's captain handed over the gunner responsible and he was:

Given his own TV show?

Adopted as a Facebook friend by the family of the man he shot?

Promptly strangled?

I think you know the answer . . .

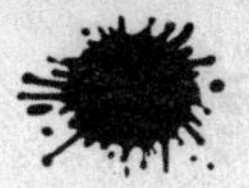

Britain's wealth was built up during the Industrial Revolution of the eighteenth and nineteenth centuries and childhood such as it was stopped at the age of 12, if not earlier, for most children.

Unless they were born into rich families, which most weren't, they were expected to help towards the family budget, often working long hours in dangerous jobs for incredibly low wages. Children were often forced to work almost as soon as they could walk. This was not something new as children had always been been expected to work. The Industrial Revolution merely accelerated and intensified the need for child labour.

In England and Scotland in 1788, two-thirds of the workers in the water-powered cotton mills were children.

Many rich families today owe their family

fortunes to the money that was made during this period of our history when child exploitation was widespread and perfectly normal. If you look up your ancestors you will probably find that most of them started working full-time well before they were teenagers and this work would have been hard, unremitting and badly paid. Working hours were long: builders worked 64 hours a week in summer and 52 in winter, while domestic servants worked 80-hour weeks. The gap between being born rich or poor was literally the difference between life and death and certainly the difference between a long, happy life and one of drudgery and danger.

The great writer Charles Dickens started work in a blacking factory when he was just 12 years old. He had no choice as his father (upon whom he based the character Mr Micawber in *David Copperfield*) was in a debtors' prison. Dickens wrote about the

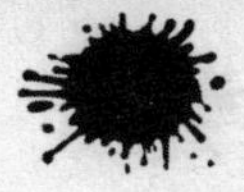

children living on the streets who stole for a living in his book, *Oliver Twist,* because he had seen it himself.

Victorian bosses prized child labour because children were cheap – orphanages were full of them – and they were easily replaced if they died or suffered permanent injury at work. Nobody complained if a few were 'lost' as there were always more waiting to be taken in. These children had no 'rights', so had to accept whatever appalling conditions they found themselves in, and if they ran away, there was nowhere for them to go. It was a wretched existence. Even those who lived with their parents were often forced to go out to work to help pay for the family's living costs.

Sometimes, children as young as four were employed in factories with dangerous – even fatal working conditions. However, it was better to work in a factory than as

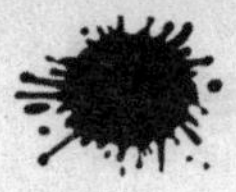

a chimney sweep. This was a vile trade that saw tiny boys – from the age of 5 or 6 – sent up large chimneys that had been blocked with soot from all the coal fires in the rooms below. The boys would come down covered in soot, and with bleeding elbows and knees. That's if they came down at all: sometimes the boys got stuck and died of suffocation.

Sometimes they would panic and freeze in fear, in which case their employer would simply light the fire underneath to 'encourage' them to get on with their work. Effectively they were driven out by the smoke or the heat or both.

In 1832 the use of boys for sweeping chimneys was forbidden by law, but it was largely ignored

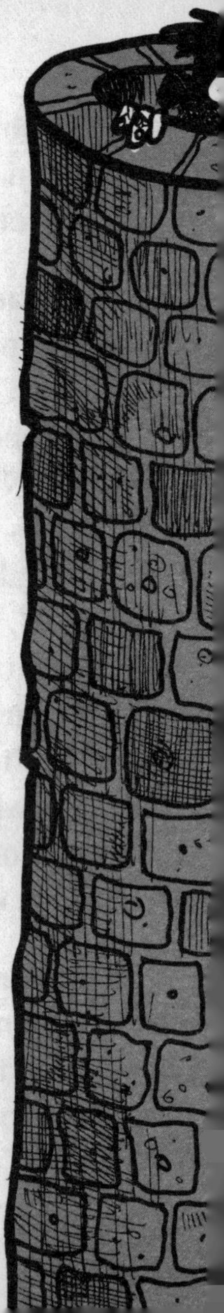

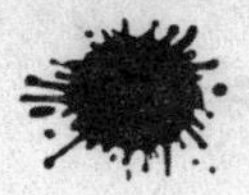

and many boys were still forced to do it.

The Water Babies by Charles Kingsley, is about a young chimney sweep named Tom, who drowns while trying to escape from his evil master, but comes to a much better life underwater as a 'water baby'.

Meanwhile, in the cotton mills, thousands of small children were employed to retrieve cotton bobbins from under the machines and to clean out cotton fluff from the intricate machinery. Some children were scalped when their hair was caught in the machine; others had their hands crushed.

Many children were killed when they went to sleep and fell into

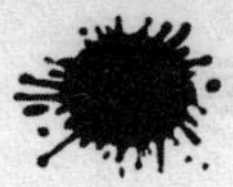

the machines, exhausted from the long hours. The noise from the machines was so loud, that people who worked in the factories often went deaf.

Then there were the coal mines where children were employed to crawl through tunnels too narrow and low for adults. This was incredibly dangerous as there were often explosions and the roof of the mine could cave in burying all the people.

The 1842 Mines Act forbade the employment of women and children in the mines.

Children also worked as errand boys, shoe blacks, making and selling matches and selling flowers and other cheap goods for which they were paid a pittance.

In the match factories children were employed to dip matches into a dangerous chemical called phosphorus. The

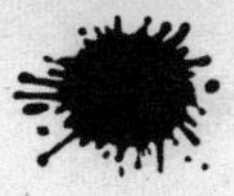

phosphorus caused their jaw bones to rot and their teeth to fall out. And some died from the effect of breathing it in.

All in all, the twentieth and twenty-first centuries have been a lot better for children than all the centuries before!

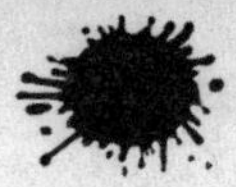

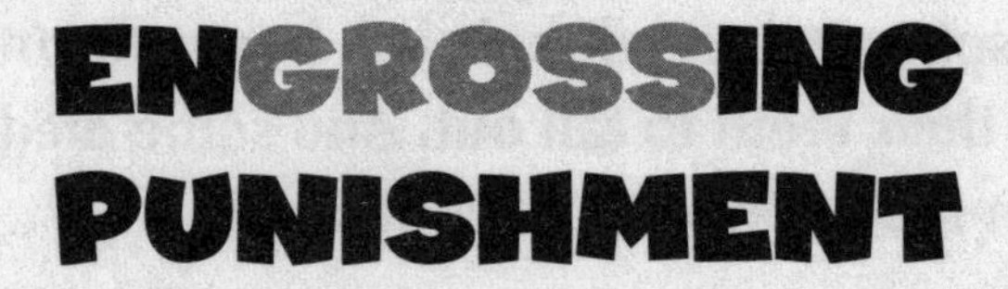

ENGROSSING PUNISHMENT

Corporal punishment – beating – was meted out to minor criminals in Britain until the practice was stopped in 1948. In the nineteenth century, public beatings for civilians and those in the armed services were extremely common.

Do you like gossip? I think most of us do – judging by the number of magazines devoted to celebrity and other sorts of gossip. But in previous centuries, gossip was seen as something to be punished. A person indulging in gossip – almost always a woman – was seen as a nuisance and labelled a 'gossip' or a 'scold'. The actual definition was 'a troublesome and angry woman who by brawling and wrangling

Did you hear
about that
Mitch Symons ?!

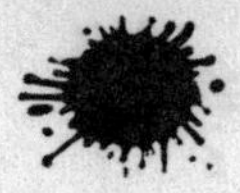

amongst her neighbours breaks the public peace, increases discord and becomes a public nuisance to the neighbourhood'.

Her punishment was to be forced to wear a scold's bridle (also called a 'brank'). This was a sort of metal mask encasing the head with a locking muzzle. There was also a small iron prong – sometimes studded with spikes that fitted in the mouth on top of the tongue to stop her from speaking. As long as she didn't try to speak, it wouldn't be painful, but it would be a source of humiliation for the woman in question for as long as she was forced to wear it – which could be for several days.

Minor crimes used to be punished by putting the perpetrator in the pillory (a wooden frame round the head and wrists) or stocks (a wooden frame securing the ankles) where he or she would be pelted with rotten fruit or, if they were unpopular, stones.

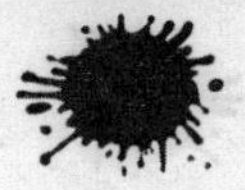

If a monk broke the law in ancient China, he'd have his neck pierced with a heavy chain, which he'd then have to drag behind him.

If sailors staged a mutiny – i.e. challenged the authority of the captain or tried to take over his ship – they could expect to be severely punished or even court martialled and executed. One particularly nasty punishment was keel-hauling, in which a prisoner would be dragged underneath the ship from one side to the other. Another was marooning, in which pirate mutineers were abandoned on an island or cast adrift on the open sea, with no provisions.

Of course, the most common punishment on ships was a flogging with a multi-tailed whip known as the cat 'o nine tails. Some crafty sailors tried to avoid punishment by having a crucifix tattooed on their backs but that rarely cut any ice with hard-hearted ships' captains.

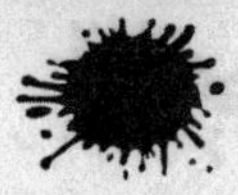

In ancient Egypt, it wasn't just the criminal who was punished, but his wife and children too: they would be cast into slavery.

In ancient China, any person who attacked a traveller had his nose cut off. This was also the punishment meted out to prisoners-of-war. In fact, it was so common that the Chinese became the first people to go in for plastic surgery to reconstruct noses.

In Ancient Rome, if a man owed money to a lot of people, they were all allowed to take a knife and cut slices off him.

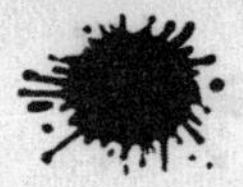

ENGROSSING TORTURE

For those of us living in the twenty-first century – and a big welcome to those of you who aren't – this next section is a little puzzling. We think that the point of torture is to extract information from someone – usually with the minimum force necessary.

It didn't use to be like that.

Oh no.

Punishment, torture, execution – they were all part of the same game*.

(*game from the point of view of the people doing the punishment, torture and execution; it is unlikely that the victims saw it in *quite* the same way . . .)

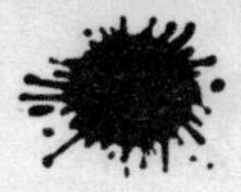

For a start, most of the time they weren't trying to find out anything meaningful from their victims. This wasn't a case of a ticking bomb and you've got the one terrorist who knows where it is. Usually, the torture was being carried out to extract a confession that the victim would have happily given without any torture. In any case, the confession wasn't necessary for a trial because, in 99 cases out of a hundred, the poor soul was going to be dead before any trial could take place.

So torture was just part of the 'judicial' process: something that took place between arrest and trial/death (whichever came first).

It was cruelty for cruelty's sake – although it is possible that some of the religious authorities that authorized the torture really did believe that confession would be good for the soul.

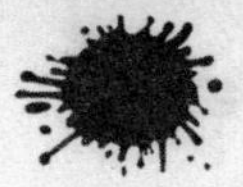

It certainly wasn't any good for the body.

As for the mind . . . well, you wonder how people didn't go mad at just the thought of it.

In fact, people did – especially if they were forced to watch someone else being tortured.

Eventually, in Britain, there came to be a distinction between torture (which was against the law), physical punishment (the stocks, whipping) and execution (designed to be effective and – relatively – humane).

But it didn't come soon enough for the poor victims of the following . . .

Crushing

The British legal system uses a lot of French and Latin words and expressions. None, however, is grislier than *peine forte et dure,* which translates from medieval French as 'hard and forceful punishment'. This was

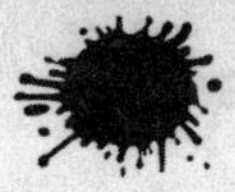

slow crushing – a cruel torture that was officially used to get defendants to plead in a court of law.

Let's say that a defendant refused to plead guilty or innocent: in other words, they just didn't speak. Technically, the law couldn't take that as a sign of guilt so the courts demanded that a person speak. That's where *peine forte et dure* came in with the defendant subjected to having heavier and heavier stones placed upon his or her chest until they either spoke or, as the weight of the stones on their chest became too great for them to breathe, they died of suffocation.

As brave as a person might be, it was hard to withstand weights of more than 150 kilos. Yet there were recorded cases where people refused to plead – even under a weight of more than 175 kilos. Their only hope was that bystanders, out of mercy, would sit on them to increase the weight

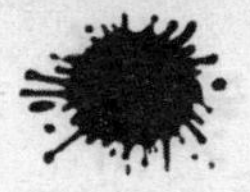

and thus speed up their deaths.

Consider then the extraordinary case of the Roman Catholic martyr Margaret Clitherow, who was pressed to death in 1586 after refusing to plead. She had been charged with hiding Catholic priests in her house, which was then against the law. Margaret knew that if there was a trial, her own children would be forced to give evidence so she simply said nothing, which meant that, effectively, there could be no trial. So the court authorized torturers to put increasing amounts of weight on her chest. She died within fifteen minutes under a weight of at least 300 kilos. No wonder the Catholic Church made her a saint.

Peine forte et dure was abolished in the UK in 1772.

The ducking stool

Although this was also used as a form of water torture for men, it was mainly used

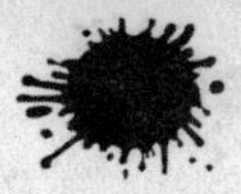

to prove (or disprove) that a woman was a witch. Here's how it worked. A woman would be tied to a chair, which was attached to a long handle. She would then be ducked in a river or a pond for a few minutes. If she didn't drown, then she was deemed to be a witch and burned at the stake. If she drowned, she was obviously not a witch but, of course, this came as little consolation to the poor woman as she had died. A clear case of 'heads I lose – tails you win'.

When the ducking stool – or variations on it – was used as a form of torture to gain confessions, the victim would be ducked until they were about to drown and then brought back up to the surface. If they failed to confess, they were ducked again until they confessed or drowned.

Foot tortures

There were many different types of foot tortures. They were used when information

I guess we won't need the stool for this one

or a confession was required but they didn't necessarily want to kill the victim. After all, a victim could take quite a lot of damage to the feet without dying.

A popular (though, curiously, not with the victim) device was a leather boot, which was put on the victim's foot. Boiling water would be poured onto the boot until it slowly got through to the victim's feet and literally melted them. A variation on this was the metal boot filled with boiling oil. You can guess the rest . . .

But who needed boots when you could simply roast a victim's feet over red-hot coals? For extra pain, lard (animal fat) could be applied to the feet first. Introduce some bellows to ratchet up the heat and you have the perfect recipe for torture. Once again, victims might have taken a different view. If this torture went the distance, the victim's feet would be totally charred and all the

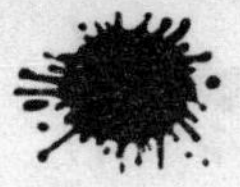

bones of the foot would drop on to the floor.

Then there was the foot press which consisted of a pair of horizontal iron plates that could be tightened around the foot and crush it completely. Sometimes, spikes were attached to the plates to make the pain even more excruciating.

The heretic's fork

This device was used by the Spanish Inquisition. It consisted of a double-ended fork with sharp prongs at each end. One end was placed under the chin, the other dug into the top of the chest making any speech impossible. But hang on a minute, what was the point of that? How can someone confess if they can't speak? To ask those (perfectly sensible) questions is again to misunderstand much of the point of medieval tortures: this was torture for torture's sake and nothing else. In fact, it was usually used *after* a confession to avoid

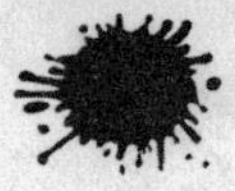

hearing the victim any further. As further evidence of this, the fork was engraved with the Latin word *abiuro* meaning ‘I recant’ (i.e. ‘I take back what I said before’) .

The iron maiden

In this sixteenth-century device, the victim was shut inside a chamber just big enough to accommodate him. Then the gruesomeness began as the door was shut and the spikes on the inside of the door pierced his body. But these spikes were cunningly placed so that they didn’t

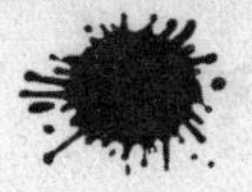

penetrate any vital organs. The torturer would open and re-close the door – making the victim stand in exactly the same place so that the spikes would re-enter his old wounds. Although this was a torture device, it's hard to believe that anyone ever survived it.

The rack

If you asked a random group of people to name a form of torture, my guess is that the most popular – i.e. common – answer would be the rack. Yet another medieval

torture device – did they do *anything* else in those days? The rack was a wooden frame with ropes fixed to the top and the bottom. The victim would be placed upon the rack and the ankles and wrists tied to the ropes. A handle was turned, which tightened the ropes, stretching the victim until they spoke – or until their limbs were literally torn apart and, presumably, they passed out with the pain.

The thumbscrew

Another torture from the Middle Ages that did precisely what it said on the packet. The torturer would take his victim's finger(s) and place it/them inside the instrument. Then he'd tighten the screw until the person confessed or their fingers were crushed.

The great advantage of the thumbscrew to the torturer was that it was very versatile: it could be used on many different parts of the body. It was also portable which meant

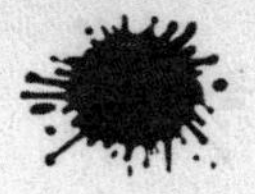

that the torturer wasn't restricted to using it in the torture chamber.
You might be interested to know that a variation on this (known as a pillwinks) was also used to straighten out children's fingers – much as we would use a brace to straighten teeth today. In fact, there's evidence to suggest that Anne Boleyn sent a pilliwinks to the nursemaid looking after her daughter, the future Queen Elizabeth I.

Water tortures

Torturers hand a tendancy to use whatever was at hand to do their ghastly work. What could be more available than water?

That's why there were many different water tortures.

The most (in)famous was the Chinese water torture, which eventually drove victims insane. The way it worked was to have constant dripping. This was either on the

victim's forehead or just near his ear. The torturer adjusted the speed and timing of the drops to mess with the human brain's tendency to make patterns of the timing or to block out the noise. This almost always led to the victim going mad.

Of course medieval British torturers were far too coarse to understand psychological torture. Their insight into the human mind only took them as far as forcing the next victim to watch a torture session. Mind you, as psychological torture goes, you've got to think that that's pretty effective. Anyway, British torturers were a lot less subtle: they would constantly drop water onto their victims to ensure physical rather than psychological harm. A constant stream of water would eventually get through the victim's skin and cause death.

Then there was ducking (see before) and variations on that theme which included

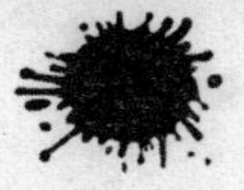

immersing a victim in freezing cold water for long periods of time or constantly pouring water over the victim's head to make him feel as if he was drowning.

Another (ab)use of water was to force the victim to drink so much that he either confessed or drowned. This was also known as the 'water cure'. The victim would have his nose clipped and then a funnel or tube stuck down his mouth through which the torturer would pour litres and litres of water. Water's good for you, but a human being can only take so much water before they die.

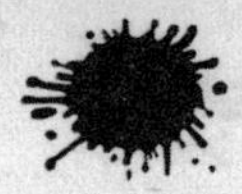

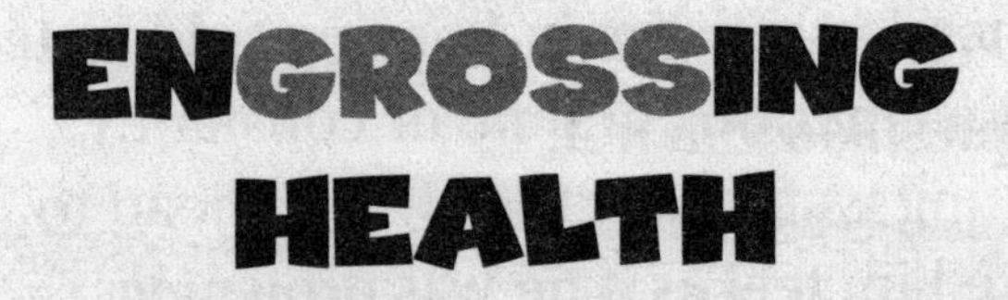

Fourteenth-century physicians didn't know what caused the plague, but they knew it was contagious. As a result they wore an early kind of bioprotective suit, which included a large beaked headpiece. The 'beak', which made them look like large birds, was filled with vinegar, sweet oils and other strong smelling compounds to counteract the stench of the dead and dying plague victims and the evil humours that they thought might be carrying the disease.

One of the remedies recommended in the fourteenth century for the Black Death was to put the intestines of young pigeons or puppies on the forehead. Other people swore by sitting in a sewer, shaving a live

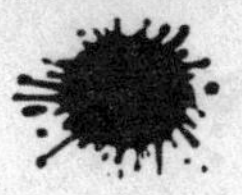

chicken's bottom and strapping it to your armpit. I kid you not.

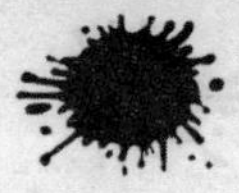

The so-called remedies for the Great Plague of 1665 were every bit as ghastly as the symptoms. They included placing a live frog on a weeping boil and putting a plucked pigeon's bottom on top of a sore. Other people, in their desperation, resorted to bursting sufferers' boils and drinking the pus. Oh that's *soooooo* gross . . .

While Europeans were dying by the thousands from smallpox, the Chinese were using a form of inoculation. They would inhale a powder made from the sores of a smallpox victim.

Before giving up on a patient they couldn't cure, doctors in the Middle East used to place their patient in the middle of town – in the (usually forlorn) hope that a passer-by might have a cure. I guess *anything* was worth trying.

No one likes bad breath and the ancient

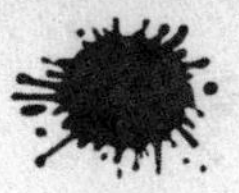

Egyptians were no different. Their remedy was slightly strange: put half a freshly killed hot mouse in the mouth. Me? I prefer mouthwash . . .

In ancient Rome, the cure for epileptic fits was to spit on the person having the fit.

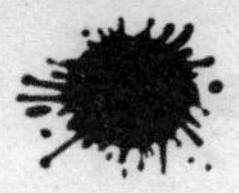

The thinking behind this seemingly unkind remedy was that this would disgust the demon possessing the victim and make him leave. Another Roman cure for epilepsy was to drink the warm blood of a newly killed gladiator.

In medieval England, a popular cure for jaundice was to swallow a live spider rolled up in butter.

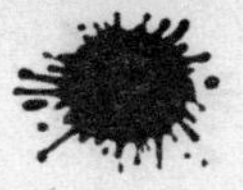

World War I saw deaths and injuries on a massive scale. It was so much worse than previous conflicts and medical staff working at the front found it almost impossible to keep up with all the casualties. So much so that soldiers who were wounded often had plugs put in their bullet holes until they could be tended to or (an unlikely occurrence given that the bullet would still be in their bodies) until their wounds had healed.

One potential medical problem that many World War I soldiers were able to avoid was toothache – but this was only because so many of them had all their teeth removed before they went to the front.

In 1914, at the start of the war, there were no dentists at all in the British Army. Then the British commander got toothache and demanded a British dentist. After that, twelve dentists were sent, but this was

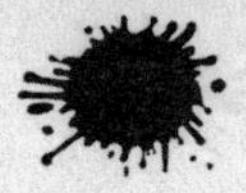

hardly enough to look after hundreds of thousands of soldiers. Therefore, it became routine for men to have all their teeth extracted beforehand and then be fitted with dentures (false teeth). In fact, from 1915 onwards, men would be passed fit for duty 'subject to dental treatment'. This meant that they were actually expected to have their teeth removed and then they'd be kept at home until their gums had healed and the dentures could be fitted. Incredible as this might sound, in fact in those days, because dentists were so expensive, many poor people had their teeth removed at the slightest sign of toothache.

In ancient Rome, people returning home from drunken parties used to throw up before going to bed in the hope/belief that it would reduce the possibility of a hangover the next morning. This was important to the ancient Romans as the standard hangover

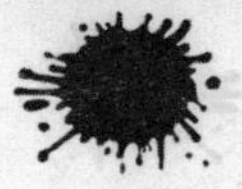

cure was to eat fried canaries, so you can see why they might want to avoid doing that. Anyway, to make themselves vomit, they'd stick feathers – usually peacock feathers – down their throats. It was thought that the Emperor Claudius died from doing this but, in fact, the feather that he used was poisoned (as were the mushrooms that he'd had for dinner).

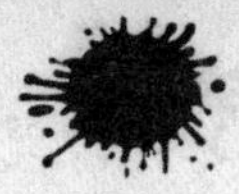

You get chilblains when your fingers or toes get very cold. In the sixteenth century, they treated them by covering them with the hot skin of a mouse. Presumably, it was similar thinking that saw people with sore throats wear pork around their necks, while teething babies would have a dead hare rubbed on their gums.

Hippocrates, who lived in the fourth century BC, is considered the father of medicine. Even today, newly qualified doctors are obliged to swear the Hippocratic Oath (named after him), in which they promise to heal patients, behave themselves and not spend *too* much time on the golf course – or something like that. Hippocrates had some strange notions. For example, he thought that violently shaking a patient cured a cough. He'd also taste samples of patients' earwax, spit, wee and even vomit. Now *that's* what I call dedication!

I fancy a nice cup of wee!
SPIT
WEE
WEE
OMIT
EARWA

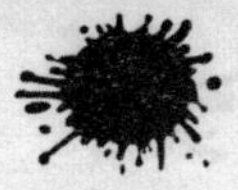

Talking of wee, ancient Chinese, Roman, and German societies frequently used it as a mouthwash. Surprisingly, the ammonia in wee is actually a good cleanser – although ancient cultures would have had no way of knowing that. Hundreds of years later, in medieval times, people with toothache were advised to gargle with wee.

In fact, fresh wee is a natural antiseptic – which is probably why the Aztecs rubbed their cuts and burns with it. Although you wouldn't really want to use another person's wee on your cut, would you?

They had some very strange ideas in the seventeenth century. Your child's got measles? No problem: send them to bed with a sheep and they'll be right as rain in the morning.

If you had a fever, the doctor would tell you to cut a pigeon in half and then wear the

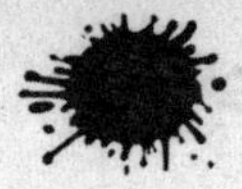

two pigeon-halves as socks. Yeah, right.

In the eighteenth and early nineteenth centuries, dentists made false teeth out of all sorts of substances, including clay and walrus tusk. Bizarre as that might seem, it was a lot better than using the teeth of soldiers killed in the battle of Waterloo or, worse still, the teeth of living children who sold them to buy food.

Traditionally, barbers' shops used to have red and white poles outside the front door. Some still do. This dates back to a time when barbers were also surgeons. But when I say surgeons, don't start imagining that they were anything like the sort we have in our modern hospitals. For a start, they weren't trained properly or qualified and very often, their idea of 'cure' would involve cutting a person's arm and letting it bleed. And all this without anaesthetic or antiseptics! The blood-stained bandages

would be wrapped around a pole outside the shop to attract more customers. Eventually, they'd just have a painted red-and-white pole. Fortunately, nowadays, barbers are restricted to cutting hair rather than arms.

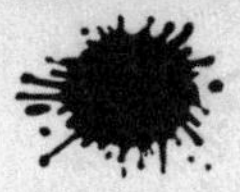

In time, properly trained surgeons replaced barbers (and locksmiths) as the people who performed operations. However, for many years (until the mid-nineteenth century), there was still no anaesthetic and so surgeons were prized for their speed more than anything else. Robert Liston was a famous Scottish surgeon who could amputate a limb in just thirty seconds.

Here are some nasty illnesses through the ages and what they were known as:

Affrighted: Frightened to death. Probably by a stress-induced heart attack

Black death: Bubonic plague

Brain fever: Meningitis

Canine madness/hydrophobia: Rabies

Chin cough: Whooping cough

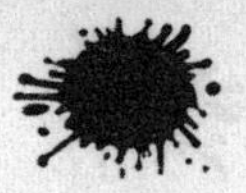

Consumption: Tuberculosis (TB)

Crop sickness: Overextended stomach

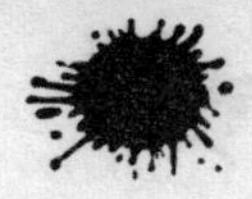

Hello Sonny,
Can you help
me cross
the road ?

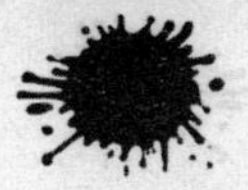

Decrepitude: Feebleness due to old age

Dropsy: Oedema (swelling), often caused by kidney or heart disease

Dry Bellyache: Lead poisoning

Elephantiasis: A form of leprosy

Flux of humour: Circulation

Gathering: A collection of pus

Grippe/grip: Influenza like symptoms

Horrors: Delirium

Jail fever/ship fever: Typhus

Lumbago: Back pain

Nostalgia: Homesickness

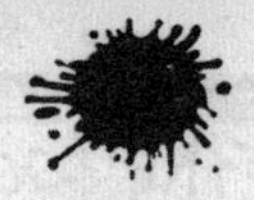

Puking fever: Milk sickness

Quinsy: Tonsillitis

Scrivener's palsy: Writer's cramp

Trench mouth: Painful ulcers found along gum line, caused by poor nutrition and poor hygiene

Winter fever: Pneumonia
In 1881, the US President James Garfield

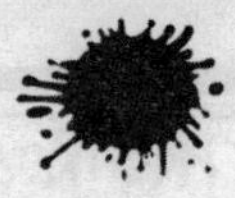

was shot twice by Charles Guiteau. One bullet grazed Garfield's arm but the second bullet was lodged somewhere in his spine and couldn't be found.

Over the next eighty days he was attended by several doctors – some of whom poked their unwashed hands into his wounds. Meanwhile, Alexander Graham Bell, the chap who invented the telephone, devised a metal detector to find the bullet, but the metal bed frame Garfield was lying on caused the metal detector to go completely haywire. It never occurred to anyone to take the poor President off the metal bed – probably because metal beds were so rare at the time.

Anyway, the upshot of all this was that President Garfield got blood poisoning followed by bronchial pneumonia and then, eighty days after the shooting, a massive heart attack. He died precisely two months short of his fiftieth birthday (which, as someone

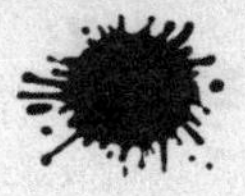

who has passed that landmark, I can tell you is not old). If only his doctors had washed their hands and used sterile instruments – and been a little more skilful – he probably would have recovered and lived a full life.

James Polk, the eleventh president of the US, was given just brandy to sedate him when he underwent gall bladder surgery at the age of 17.

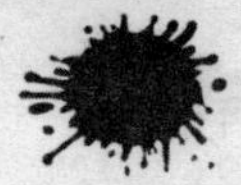

ENGROSSING CANNIBALISM

There are two distinct reasons for cannibalism. The first is need. If you're in a plane that's crashed in the Andes (as actually happened) or in a life-raft in the middle of the ocean (ditto – many times), then you might be forced to eat your fellow human beings in order to stay alive.

I think most of us can understand that.

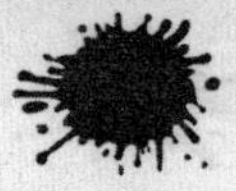

We might be less understanding of tribes that ate human flesh because meat was scarce. A vegetarian diet might be limited and boring, but is surely preferable to eating people.

In other words, cannibalism can be justified in extreme cases where simple survival depends on it.

The second reason is as a lifestyle or cultural choice. For instance when it's done in the name of sacrifice to some god or other or to seal a victory over a vanquished enemy. Talking of which, did you know that an exocannibal is a cannibal that eats only enemies while an endocannibal eats only friends, or at least fellow tribe members?

That would make the people of Papua New Guinea (at least before the twentieth century) endocannibals as they used to eat

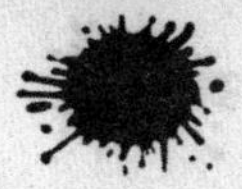

the bodies of dead relatives – as a mark of respect.

Mind you, they weren't that picky. In 1859 a ship, the *Saint Paul*, was on its way to Australia when it was shipwrecked near one of the islands of Papua New Guinea. The islanders cooked and ate all but one of the 326 passengers. I wonder why they didn't eat the 326th? Perhaps they were full!

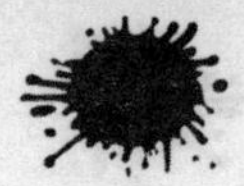

ENGROSSING FUN

Inventors apply for patents in order to protect their inventions. Of course, not every invention leads to a product. One such invention was Adolf A. Neubauer's 1900 plan for a device that fixed to the saddle of a bicycle to deter thieves. It was a spike that shot out from the saddle and stabbed the would-be thief in the bum. Funnily enough, it never took off! A similar idea was used by Frank P. Snow when he devised his hat protector in 1914. It had a spike in the rim. Yup, that should work.

In the fourteenth and fifteenth centuries, people used to use animal dung when building their homes.

YEOOOW!

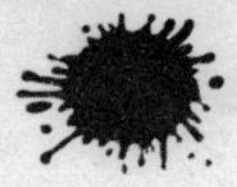

When the sixteenth-century Danish astronomer Tycho Brahe lost the bridge of his nose in a duel (during his student days) he replaced it with one made of a mixture of silver and gold.

In the days before toilet paper became readily available, people just had to use er, whatever came to hand. In the United States during the late nineteenth century, the catalogue for the Sears department store was very popular with bottom-wipers because it was printed on lovely soft paper. So guess what happened when Sears started printing on hard, shiny paper? Sales of the catalogue went down!

Toilet paper shortages aren't just a matter of ancient history. As recently as 1994, there was a severe shortage in communist Cuba. After everyone had used up their newspapers, magazines and telephone directories, they started stealing books

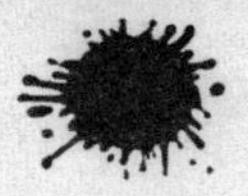

– even rare ones – from libraries. If you borrowed this book from a library, I'd be grateful if you only used it for the intended purpose.

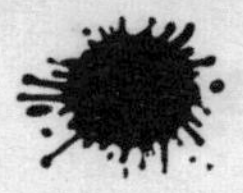

Of course, there was no need for toilet paper – or books – if you were an Egyptian pharaoh because you would have your very own royal bottom wiper . . . or, indeed, if you were a king. Up to the sixteenth century, many European palaces had an official 'Groom of the Stool' whose job was to wipe the king's bottom. Obviously, there was no toilet paper so the royal bottom wipers had to use their hands.

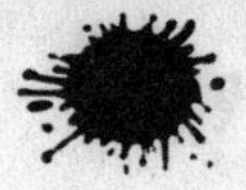

Talking of Egyptian pharaohs . . . Pharaoh Pepi II kept several naked slaves around him whose bodies he had smeared with honey. This encouraged flies to land on them instead of him. No wonder he lived until he was 94 years old!

Such was her power as a 'fashionista' that when Marie Antoinette, an eighteenth-century queen of France, became pregnant, all the fashionable women of Paris started wearing padding over their stomachs. As her pregnancy developed, the women wore thicker and thicker pads. When her baby was born, the women's fashions all returned to normal.

A Bible published in 1631 contained the unfortunate commandment: 'Thou shalt commit adultery'. The printers were fined the then HUGE sum of £300 and went out of business – just for missing out the word 'not'. Understandably, it became known

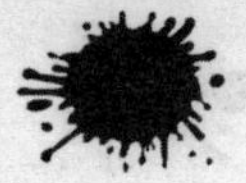

as The Wicked Bible.

What goes around comes around. The first man to be locked in the stocks was the man who invented them. Similarly, the inventor of a cage that fits just one person (with no room to move or sit down) was the only person to be locked in it. You've got to laugh!

A student in ancient Athens came up with a clever way to force himself to stick to his studies. He shaved off half the hair on his head. Then when he was tempted to go out, he would remember his appearance and be too embarrassed and so would stay home and study instead.

In 1325, the Italian city states of Bologna and Modena went to war over a stolen bucket. The Battle of Zappolino – which was won by the Modenese – is also known as the War of the Oaken Bucket.

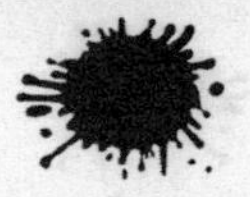

One of the artist and inventor Leonardo da Vinci's inventions was a stink bomb mounted on an arrow.

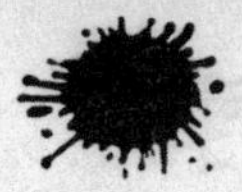

According to the writer John Aubrey in his book *Brief Lives*, Edward de Vere, seventeenth Earl of Oxford, was bowing particularly low to Queen Elizabeth I one day when he accidentally broke wind. So embarrassed was he that he went into voluntary exile for seven years. Eventually he returned to court and once again found himself in the presence of the queen. He

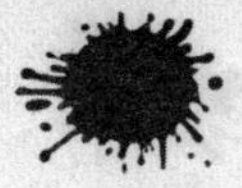

bowed carefully this time. The intense silence was only broken by Elizabeth commenting, 'My Lord, I had forgot the fart.'

King Henri IV was one of the most popular French kings, both during and after his reign (from 1589–1610). He showed great care for the welfare of his subjects and displayed an unusual religious tolerance for those days. However, that's not why he appears in this book. No, he's here because he was described as 'smelling like carrion'. When his fiancée met him for the first time, she fainted because of his smell!

The Incas used to punish rebels by killing them and making musical instruments out of their bones.

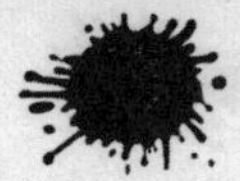

ENGROSSING FOOD

In 1868, a banquet was held in London where the main course was horse – more than 130 kilos of it.

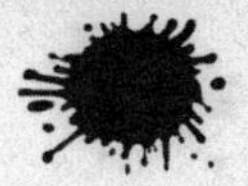

You get scurvy if you don't eat fruit and vegetables. You might be surprised to know that King Henry VIII suffered from scurvy. Why? Because in the sixteenth century, wealthy people ate meat – vegetables were supposedly for peasants. And so Henry got scurvy. Shows the importance of a balanced diet.

Kings and queens often had food-tasters so that they wouldn't get poisoned (no, the food-taster would instead!). King Charles VIII of France, however, was so completely terrified by the thought of being poisoned that he wouldn't rely on food-tasters and simply stopped eating and drinking. Eventually, he died – not from poison but from malnutrition.

Nowadays we know about the dangers of lead but in olden days they didn't. So women in Tudor times died from wearing make-up containing lead, while the ancient

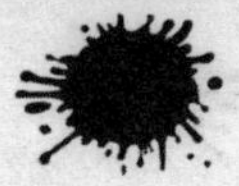

Romans fatally consumed leaded grape pulp and leaded wine.

As you know, the French eat frogs and snails, but these only became 'delicacies' – i.e. foods for the posh – in the seventeenth century.

In the nineteenth century, people used to chew paraffin wax the way people chew gum these days.

Nero, the infamous Roman Emperor, had a slave whose job it was to be a 'glutton'. Sounds great, doesn't it? Except when you realize that the slave had to eat everything that was put in front of him. And what made it worse than I'm A Celebrity...Get Me Out Of Here!, was that he also had to eat human flesh.

ENGROSSING – UNBELIEVABLE

I don't know if this is true, but it's such a great story that I'm going to tell it anyway. On April 18, 1599, a church steeple in Germany was struck by lightning and destroyed. It was rebuilt but, over the next two hundred years, it was hit by lightning three more times – each lightning strike occurring on an April 18.

The teenage Roman Emperor Elagabalus was incredibly cruel and, not to put too fine a point on it, absolutely bonkers. This was an alarming combo. He used to order mass human sacrifices of young boys and girls and demanded that his priests present him with golden bowls full of children's intestines. He once ordered a servant to

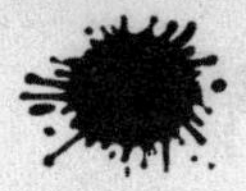

fetch him a big packet of cobwebs (like you do). When the unfortunate servant failed to find any cobwebs, Elagabalus had him locked up in a cage and eaten alive by hundreds of starving rats. When he held a dinner party, he decided to have rose petals dropped from the ceiling. Now that doesn't sound too cruel, does it? But he had so many rose petals dropped that many of his dinner guests were suffocated to death. Still, he got his just deserts: when he was 18, his enemies found him in a toilet and stabbed him to death.

In nineteenth-century Europe, there was a 'fashion' for human exhibits. The German showman, Carl Hagenbeck, exhibited humans described as 'savages', including Inuit and native African peoples, in his Hamburg zoo.

Twelfth-century European emperors were the celebrities of their day. Everything they

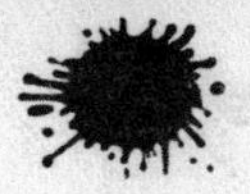

did and everywhere they went was under the spotlight. When, in 1184, the Holy Roman Emperor Frederick Barbarossa met with his nobles, so many of them followed him into the toilet that the floor gave way. The emperor saved himself by grabbing the iron bars of the window, but many others fell to their death.

When the Byzantine emperor Justinian II was deposed in 695AD, his enemies slit his nose and tongue on the basis that he

would never be able to rule again if he were disfigured. They couldn't have been more wrong. Ten years later, Justinian the Slit-nosed returned to power and paraded his enemies through the streets before killing them.

In 1347, besiegers of a Turkish city flung plague-infected bodies over the walls of the city to make it surrender. This early example of biological warfare helped to introduce the Black Death into Europe.

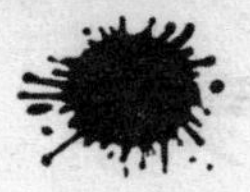

In Greek mythology, the Cyclops was a giant with a single eye in the middle of his forehead. In France, in the late eighteenth century, lived a girl who had a single eye in the middle of her face.

When Roman gladiators weren't fighting each other, they were fighting wild animals – especially lions. Unfortunately, so many lions were taken from North Africa that they became extinct in that part of the world.

The Vikings believed that the first people came from the sweat of a giant's armpits. They also believed that the sky was held up by four dwarves called North, South, East and West.

Talking of Vikings, you'll have heard the word berserk used to mean mad or barmy. It comes from the Norse (i.e. the Viking language) for 'bear shirt' because the berserkers, legendary Norse warriors

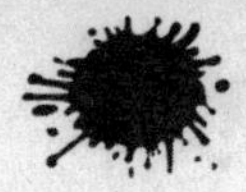

who fought like madmen, went into battle wearing shirts made of bear skins.

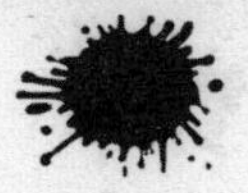

However, they were complete wusses compared to Celt warriors who went into battle completely naked.

Genghis Khan, the twelfth-century founder of the Mongol Empire (the largest joined-up empire in history) was not only cruel, but cunning. When he laid siege to one city, he demanded that the city's inhabitants supplied him with thousands of cats and swallows. He then tied flaming cloths to their tails and set them free – whereupon they went back to the city and set fire to it.

King Charles I was executed in 1649. Two centuries later, Sir Walter Scott, the novelist who wrote *Ivanhoe*, managed somehow to get hold of one of the king's neck vertebrae and used it as a salt cellar.

Buddhism is a religion that forbids the harming of any living creature – even insects. This presented Chinese emperors

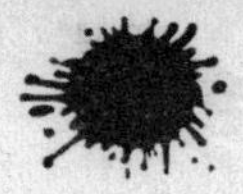

with certain problems. One sixth-century emperor got around it in a very cunning way. If he had to kill someone, he fitted them with bamboo wings and made them try to fly. Obviously they couldn't and died. This emperor killed over 700 rivals in a single year using this method.

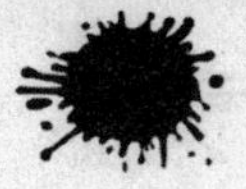

King Charles VI of France started off his reign known as 'Charles the Beloved' which was a pretty good beginning. Alas, by the time of his death in 1422, he was known as 'Charles the Mad'. The clue was in the name. For example, he became convinced that his body was made of glass. Yes, *glass*. In fact, so convinced was he of this 'fact', he refused to allow people to touch him, and wore reinforced clothing to protect himself from accidental 'shattering'.

In Mayan culture (which was big in Central America around the first few centuries AD), children were encouraged to cut themselves with stingray-tails so that they could sacrifice their blood to the gods.

Here's an incredible story. During World War 1, a German soldier was riding in the back seat of a plane when the engine suddenly stalled and he fell out of his seat. Parachutes weren't used in military aircraft

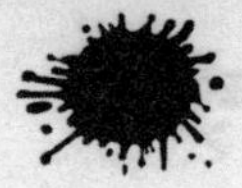

and, being two miles above the ground, he would almost certainly have died. However – and this is the remarkable bit – as he was falling, the plane started falling too and he was blown back into his own seat. The pilot, who'd managed to remain in the plane all along, was able to land the plane safely.

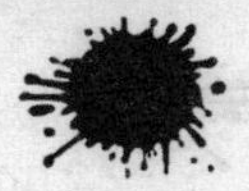

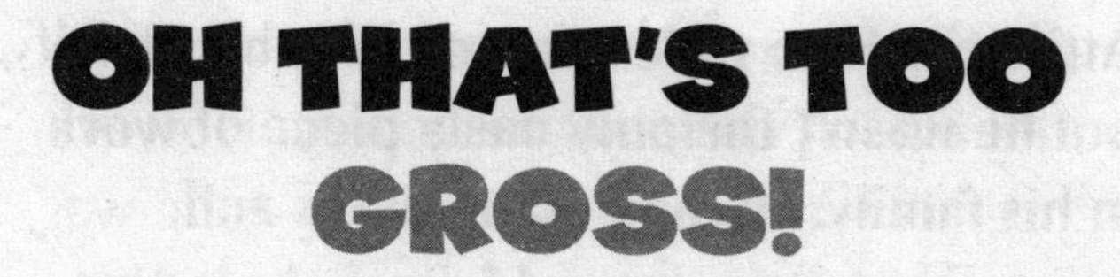

In ancient Rome, they used to use urine to clean laundry. Believe it or not, it's an effective bleach! To make sure they had a regular supply (wee, not laundry), people would leave containers in the street for other people to pee in.

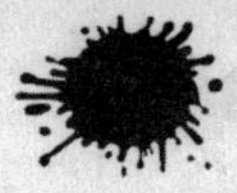

Attila the Hun was renowned for his cruelty, but he wasn't the only nasty piece of work in his family. He had many wives and, according to one legend loosely based on his life, when one of them was annoyed with him (not unreasonably as he had murdered her brothers), she murdered two of his other wives' children and served up their hearts to him for his dinner.

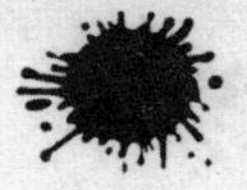

When the Spanish were trying to capture and colonize Mexico, they accidentally spread smallpox among the locals. After a while, they decided that this was a good thing because it reduced the number of their enemies and so they began to introduce the deadly disease *deliberately*.

The Aztecs believed that the tears of children would make the rains come and improve their harvest. Unfortunately, there was no one to tell them that they were bonkers and so they put children in mountain caves to make them cry – sometimes letting them starve to death. And, no, it didn't have any effect on the weather . . .

The fourteenth-century leader Tamerlane played polo with the skulls of people he had killed in battle. But that was nothing compared to what he did to the Persian city of Isfahan after the people revolted

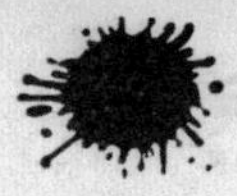

against his terrible taxes. He had the entire population of 70,000 people massacred. He and his men left behind 28 towers of skulls piled up outside the city walls – each tower consisting of about 1,500 skulls.

When Mary Queen of Scots was executed, it took three attempts to cut off her head. The first attempt only partially severed her head. Mind you, if often took lots of blows before a head could be properly hacked off. It was for this reason that people about to be beheaded gave a tip to their executioner, to make it as swift and as painless as possible.

Many old Celtic graves contain the bodies of an old person and several younger people. Archaeologists think that the younger people were killed as a sacrifice to keep the old person company in the next life.

Meanwhile, Saxon wives were sometimes

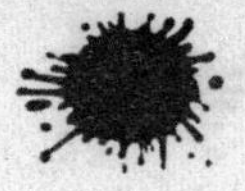

buried alive with their husbands to keep them company in the afterlife.

The Holy Roman Emperor Frederick II was an unusually intelligent man for his times (the twelfth century). His contemporaries called him 'the wonder of the world' and he had the decency to ban trials by ordeal – on the basis that the stronger man always won, whether he was guilty or not. However, his curiosity took him into very dubious areas. For instance, he studied the human digestive system by murdering his dinner guests.

Then he put a prisoner in a cask because he wanted to see the man's soul escaping though a hole in the cask when the prisoner died. Perhaps his nastiest experiment was when he fed two prisoners and then sent one out to hunt and the other one to bed. That would have been OK but the next part wasn't: he then had them disemboweled –

just to see which one of them had digested their meal better.

When Genghis Khan died in 1227, he was buried beneath a tree near his birthplace. His soldiers killed all witnesses to the funeral (including animals) then killed themselves so that no living being would know where he was buried.

The last executions in Britain were in 1964 – although the death penalty itself wasn't abolished until the following year. Actually, that's not strictly accurate. It was abolished for murder in 1965 and then for treason and piracy in 1998. The important thing is that no one's been executed here for getting on for fifty years.

It wasn't always like that though. In fact you only have to go back to the 19th century to find the death penalty handed out for an extraordinary range of 'crimes' – including

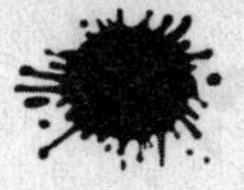

some that we wouldn't even recognize as crimes these days.

Interestingly, there had 'only' been some fifty capital offences in the early 18th century but these had increased to an extraordinary 222 offences a hundred years later. No wonder it became known as the 'Bloody Code'. These 222 offences that saw over ten thousand Britons hanged included:

Appearing on the highway (ie. on a road) with a sooty face (the assumption being that the person was a burglar).

Associating with gypsies (for longer than a month).

Cutting down a tree.

Damaging a fish pond.

Damaging Westminster Bridge (just graffiti would be enough).

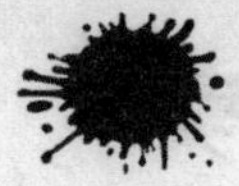

Impersonating a pensioner of Greenwich Hospital.

Pickpocketing

Poaching (trapping and killing a wild animal on someone else's land)

Setting fire to a hayrick.

Stealing anything worth more than five shillings (25p- or £30 in today's values).

Stealing from a shipwreck

Stealing livestock (sheep, cows etc.)

If, like me, you live in the UK, you might be interested to know that in the 19th century, Wiltshire, Hereford and Essex executed the greatest number of people, while the courts in Yorkshire, Durham and Lancashire executed the fewest.

You might think that once you were hanged that was the end of the punishment but, no it wasn't. First of all, anyone executed would be buried in unconsecrated (i.e. unblessed) ground which would be terrible for those

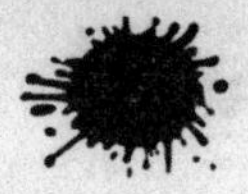

with a strong Christian faith.

Then there was gibbeting, a post mortem (ie. after death) punishment used for such people as highwaymen and pirates. After they had been hanged, their bodies were taken down and then coated in pitch. They were then put into iron cages and suspended by a chain from the gibbet which would be sited somewhere prominent – like at the top of a hill.

The bodies would then be left for several months – or even years – until they had rotted away, thus serving as a warning to others.

Even if you committed an offence that didn't carry the death sentence, the punishments could still be terribly severe. In 1791, a 63-year-old woman named Sarah Douglas stole some table linen. Nowadays, she'd receive a caution and be sent on her way. Instead, she was transported to New

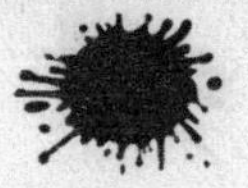

South Wales (Australia) for seven years. At her age, I very much doubt that she ever returned.

Similarly, in 1874, a man named John Walker was sentenced to seven years in prison for stealing a few onions.

The Romans specialized in devising ever new and ghastly means of execution. One such was to cover a victim in honey and have them stung to death by wasps.

Actually, I think they might have got that one from the Ancient Persians who used something called Scaphism (also known as 'the boats'). A person would be fastened in a back-to-back pair of narrow rowing boats (or a hollowed-out tree trunk), with their head, hands and feet hanging out. They would then have honey rubbed on their body to attract insects to their exposed parts before being left to float on a stagnant pond. The twist on this particularly horrible form of execution is that the poor victim would be given plenty of food and drink so that not only did they carry on living (to suffer more) but the resulting poo would attract even more insects...

The Cave Of Roses was a 17th century Swedish method of execution in which

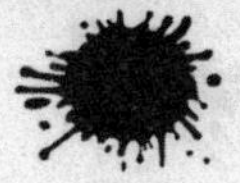

prisoners were put into a cave of poisonous snakes.

Exposure doesn't sound like a means of execution but it could be when it was inflicted for a long period of time. Although exposure was sometimes used as a short punishment, it was usually intended to kill the person – especially if they were buried up to their neck rather than merely left outside for a long period of time. It also had the merit – from the point of view of the people inflicting the punishment – of being incredibly cheap.

If exposure wasn't enough, then there was also the option, in winter, of freezing a person to death. Here, the naked victim would be made to stand outside and have icy cold water poured on them which would freeze – thereby making him die slowly and painfully.

Slow slicing – or the death by a thousand cuts - was a form of execution used in China for a thousand years from 900AD. Here, the condemned person was killed as slowly as possible one slice at a time. Inevitably, most of the cuts happened after death which might not seem like much of a punishment to us but the thought of it would have tormented the victim because they wouldn't be whole in the next life.

Although boiling alive was stopped in England in the 16th century, it was employed by the 19th century Madagascan Queen Ranavalona as one of many gross

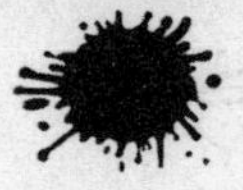

punishments that this most cruel of queens inflicted on her enemies.

In 19th century Mongolia, prisoners were executed by being nailed into wooden boxes (in reality, coffins) and left out on the prairies to die of exposure and starvation.

When you think of cowboys dying, you immediately think of gunfights. In fact, the most common cause of death was being dragged by a horse because their spurs (the things they used to make the horses go faster) got caught in the saddle's stirrups.

Another man who was boiled to death – but this time in oil – was Pomponio Algerio, an Italian law student, in 1556. He was killed simply because he believed he had the right to free speech – something that the Roman Inquisition wouldn't accept. He took fifteen minutes to die but was said to have maintained his composure and dignity throughout. What a hero!

Turn over to see
sneak peeks from another
THAT'S SO
GROSS!
BOOKS

MITCHELL SYMONS
THAT'S SO
GROSS!
HUMAN
BODY
FREE
COLLECTOR
CARDS
INSIDE

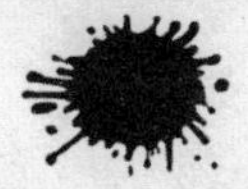

ENGROSSING SWEAT

Why do we sweat? Basically, our bodies work best when we are about 37 degrees Celsius, but in hot weather or hot rooms or if we exercise or dress too warmly, we heat up higher than that. If that continued, we wouldn't be able to tolerate heat and our bodies would eventually explode from over-heating.

Luckily, the body has ways to deal with overheating. A part of your brain called the hypothalamus helps control temperature. When you start to get too hot, it sends an urgent message to sweat glands – of which there are millions all over our bodies – to start making sweat (also known as perspiration). This leaves your skin through tiny holes called pores. Sweat is made of water, salt and sugar. When it hits the air, it starts to evaporate (this means it turns from a liquid to a vapour). As the sweat evaporates off your skin, you cool down.

Sweat is a great cooling system, but if you're

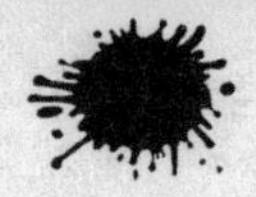

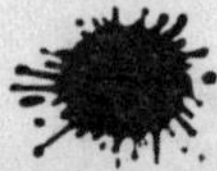

sweating a lot on a hot day, or after playing hard, you could be losing too much water through your skin. Then you need to put liquid back in your body by drinking plenty of water so you don't get dehydrated.

Sweat by itself doesn't smell at all. It's the bacteria that live on your skin that mix with the sweat and give it a stinky smell. So it's stale sweat – rather than sweat itself – that smells. And sweaty unwashed clothes can really honk! Fortunately, regular washing with soap and water keeps most of us fresh and nice to be near. However, when you reach puberty, special hormones affect the glands in your armpits, and these glands make some individuals smellier than others: these people may need a gentle hint to wash more, or use products that will help them become nicer to be around.

Men usually have much more active sweat glands than women.

You don't sweat evenly under each arm. Right-handed people sweat more under their left arm while left-handers get sweatier under their right arm.

MITCHELL SYMONS
THAT'S SO
GROSS!
ANIMALS
FREE
COLLECTOR
CARDS
INSIDE

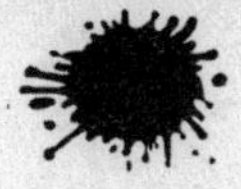

ENGROSSING - UNUSUAL

One in 5,000 North Atlantic lobsters is born bright blue.

The male seahorse – rather than the female seahorse – carries the eggs, inside a pouch on its stomach.

During the reign of Kublai Khan in the 13th century, the Chinese used lions on hunting expeditions. They trained the big cats to pursue and drag down massive animals – from wild bulls to bears – and to stay with the kill until the hunters arrived.

Wombats roam across an area of up to four hectares around their warren. Unlike most mammals, however, it's the young females who leave the area where they were born, while the males stay put.

Flying frogs change colour at different times of the day and night. During the day, they're greenish-blue then; as twilight falls, they turn

green, but when it gets dark, they turn black.

Spotted skunks do handstands before they spray.

In the Caribbean there are oysters that can climb trees.

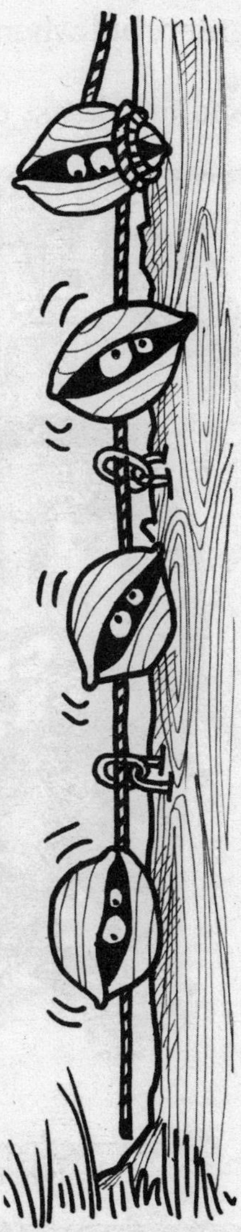

Because it has no backbone, a 35-kilo octopus can squeeze through a hole the size of a large coin.

The thorny devil, a lizard that is native to Australia, lives in very dry conditions. It drinks by channelling tiny dewdrops that collect on its skin at night along surface grooves to its mouth.

To keep cool, ostriches pee on their legs.

Jellyfish sometimes evaporate if stranded on a beach–they are 98 per cent water.

Sharks have six senses. Besides vision, hearing, touch, taste and smell, they can also sense the tiny amounts of electricity given off by other animals.

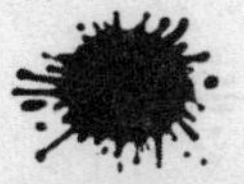

MITCHELL SYMONS
THAT'S SO GROSS!
CREEPY CRAWLIES
FREE COLLECTOR CARDS INSIDE

ENGROSSING STRENGTH

The strongest insect is the rhinoceros beetle, which is so powerful it can carry 850 times its own weight – which would be like you trying to carry a jumbo jet on your back. Don't try this at home – always assuming that you keep a jumbo jet in your back garden . . .

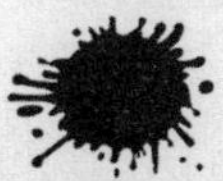